Fine Motor ABC

Alphabet Themed Activities to Strengthen Fine Motor Skills

Stacie Erfle, MS, OTR/L

Also in the ABC Series:

Gross Motor ABC
Sensory ABC

ISBN-10: 0-692-67958-8
ISBN-13: 978-0-692-67958-6

A Note to Parents

Build skills one page at a time with Fine Motor ABC; 26 targeted activities to develop foundational and functional fine motor skills.

Each activity in the book is accompanied by a photograph showing how to perform the task, corresponding alphabet hand sign, and two sections of text. The main text is a rhyming couplet written in children's book style. It is a quick, fun, and engaging description of the activity. This gets kids interested and gives simple vocabulary to use when completing or discussing each task. The bottom text is designed to give teachers, parents, and caregivers more information about what the activity is addressing and its importance. This empowers adults with the knowledge of not only what to do to help kids develop skills, but how to do it, and why.

Whether you simply read through the book, do all 26 activities in a row, or something in between, know that each time a child interacts with Fine Motor ABC they are building skills for success.

Stacie Erfle, MS, OTR/L

Stacie Erfle, MS, OTR/L

www.skillbuilderbooks.com

Aa

Move like an animal – bear crawl or crab walk.
Growl like a grizzly, but does a crab talk?

Upper extremity weight bearing prior to fine motor tasks provides input to the muscles and joints of the hands, arms, and shoulders. Called proprioceptive input, this facilitates body awareness and encourages coordinated movements.

Bb

Create a pattern when putting beads on a string.
Make it repeat until you finish the whole thing.

The ability for the eyes and hands to work together effectively is called visual-motor integration or eye-hand coordination. It is foundational to all paper and pencil tasks, and is also required for activities such as stringing beads and catching a ball.

Cc

Curve your hand to make a **cup**.
Find some coins and fill it up.

Curving the hand develops the longitudinal arch. The arches of the hand make it possible to hold objects of various sizes and shapes.

Dd

Just like sewing, lace the string up and **down**.
Use any color – red, green, blue, or brown.

To support the development of hand dominance, a child should be encouraged to not switch hands during an activity. For example, if they start using their right hand to lace and their left hand to hold the lacing card, they should complete the task in that manner.

Ee

Left and right thumbs up, now cut on the line.
Sit up tall and keep your elbows close to your spine.

Effective positioning of the hands and body is required for successful performance of fine motor activities. Poor positioning makes a task more difficult and can impair a child's ability to develop age-appropriate skills.

Ff

Use your thumb and 2 fingers to make O's.
You can do it with your hands but not with your toes.

This position creates space between the thumb and index finger, called an open web space. It requires adequate strength and stability in the muscles of the thumb. When the web space is closed, the thumb is held against the side of the index finger, limiting a functional fingertip grasp.

Gg

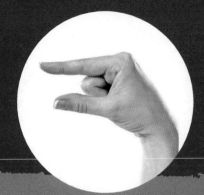

Peel the paper off broken crayons and then hold the tip.
Using just your fingers will improve your **grip**.

A short crayon or pencil limits the opportunity for children to use atypical grasp patterns such as wrapping all fingers up the length of the writing tool.

Hh

Draw a picture - you can kneel, sit, or stand.
Just don't forget to hold the paper with your helping hand.

Bilateral integration is the ability to coordinate the two sides of the body. One way this is done is by using the non-dominant helping hand to stabilize materials while the dominant working hand performs a task.

Ii

Make an 8 lying down, **imagine** it's fast asleep.
Trace over it 10 times without making a peep.

Crossing over the midline, or middle, of the body is required to develop hand dominance. Having a highly skilled, dominant hand is needed for fine motor skills such as handwriting. If a child writes with both hands, each hand will not have adequate practice opportunities to become efficient.

Jj

Hold onto a treasure with 2 fingers tight.
Your other 3 fingers can hold the pencil **just** right.

The most common way to hold a pencil is a tripod grasp, using the thumb, index finger, and middle finger. Although this is ideal, there are many variations. The most important component is that the pencil grasp is functional and can produce writing with sufficient legibility and speed.

Kk

Move 5 pennies from fingertips to palm.
Try to keep them all in your hand, it's tricky, stay calm.

This kind of movement is referred to as translation. It is an example of in-hand manipulation, the ability to move objects using only one hand. These types of complex fine motor skills allow for effective object positioning.

Ll

Glue dried beans on the letters of your name.
Or do the whole alphabet and make it a game.

When picking up small items with the thumb and tip of the index finger, a child is using a pincer grasp. This grasp begins to develop in infancy and is needed for everything from self-feeding to holding a pencil.

Mm

With tweezers or tongs move raisins around.
But please don't put them where they can't be found.

Grasp and release activities, such as tongs and spray bottles, develop the open and close
motion required for using scissors.

Nn

Build a paperclip chain link by link.
It could be a **necklace**, what do you think?

Not all fine motor activities need to be done at a table. A great alternative position that builds shoulder strength and stability is lying on the belly using the elbows to prop up the body. This position, called prone, can be used when drawing, doing puzzles, and manipulating small objects.

Oo

Tap your fingers **one** at a time.
Now you're playing the piano, just like a mime.

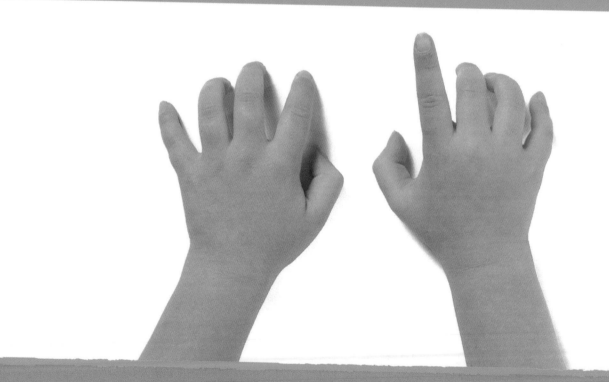

The ability to move fingers one at a time is called finger isolation. Fine motor skills require that the hand does not move as a unit, but that the fingers can work individually.

Pp

Use your thumb, **pointer**, and tall man to open a clothespin. Clip them to paper or the edge of a bin.

Tucking the ring and pinky fingers into the palm provides a stable base that allows the thumb, index finger, and middle finger to make precise movements. Known as hand separation, it is required for numerous fine motor skills including writing and cutting.

Qq

Turn into a plank, make your body a straight line.
Hold it for 10, don't quit, you're doing fine.

Postural control, the ability to maintain an upright body position, and shoulder strength are necessary for fine motor skills. A child with poor postural control will often tire easily when seated and will compensate by lying on or leaning against the table.

Rr

Roll out a long snake with some playdough.
Pinch from the head to the tail, left to right, and go slow.

Pinching with the thumb, index finger, and middle finger strengthens the muscles needed for a tripod grasp. Playdough can also be squeezed, flattened, pounded, and squashed for hand strengthening.

Ss

Crumple paper with your fingertips into a ball. Make 5 big and then make 5 small.

Strength and stability are both needed for efficient fine motor skills. Forming paper into a ball can strengthen the fingers; however, ensure that the thumb maintains a stable position and does not collapse at the base or pinch against the side of the index finger.

Tt

Find a cap and give it a **twirl**.
Pretend it's as precious as a clam with a pearl.

Rotating an object at the fingertips develops in-hand manipulation. Other examples include twirling a pencil and pushing a button through the hole. In-hand manipulation skills require thumb to finger opposition, the ability for the tip of the thumb to touch the tips of the fingers.

Uu

Color with your paper **up** on the wall.
Use plenty of tape so that it won't fall.

When working on a vertical surface, the wrist is naturally put into extension, with the back of the hand closer to the arm. This allows for improved thumb positioning and finger movements. Additionally, it inhibits wrist flexion, which is often used to compensate for poor wrist stability.

Vv

Use a **variety** of shapes to draw a person and frog. Then add the setting, some grass and a log.

Drawing pictures not only supports literacy development, but builds a foundation for handwriting skills. A child should be able to copy basic geometric shapes such as circles, plus signs, squares and triangles before they are expected to write letters.

Ww

Make shadow puppets on the wall or floor.
A rabbit and spider, can you think of more?

Placing the hands into novel positions requires motor planning, the ability to figure out how to do an unfamiliar movement. Motor planning is needed for fine motor control and allows children to learn new tasks.

Xx

Sign the alphabet, a to x y z.
Start at the beginning, that is the key.

In addition to developing fine motor skills, sign language provides a kinesthetic, or physical, approach to learning the alphabet. The varied hand positions help to develop the arches of the hand, thumb opposition, hand separation, and finger isolation.

Yy

Pinch and rip to tear paper apart.
Glue down the pieces to create your own art.

Ensure that children are given the opportunity to use their creativity when doing fine motor projects. Giving them the freedom to create their own work instead of directly copying an example can increase interest and encourage participation.

Zz

Button, zip, tie, and snap.
Once you're done, give yourself a clap.

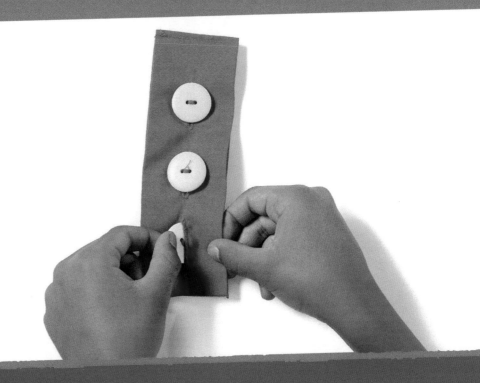

Practicing fine motor tasks within the context of a functional activity is the best way to develop skills and build independence. In addition to these fastener tasks, a child can work on functional hand skills by opening and closing containers such as jars, toothpaste tubes, and plastic zip bags.

Made in the USA
Charleston, SC
15 July 2016